THE HAPPINESS WORKBOOK:

RISE UP, HAPPINESS

SOLDIERS

Christina Unrein

ACKNOWLEDGMENTS

I had so much support in completing this book! Everywhere I turned, I was supported by my friends and family! I want to give special thank you's to these awesome people:

Adam – Thank you for your perspective, feedback, and encouragement! Knowing that some of the ideas I am sharing are novel and others are on track with positive psychology is very helpful!

Amy – Thank you for great explanations on what you thought of the book and ideas to make it better!

Andrew – Thank you for challenging me to expand many of the ideas and to give more details! Your perspective reminded me that not providing information can help some become curious. ☺

Ariel – Thank you for reviewing the book and confirming that it was doable and FUN!

Evie – Thank you for telling me that the cover needs to reflect the great content better, detailing all your thoughts as you reviewed, and for always being willing to help!

Judy – Thank you for your detailed feedback, encouragement, and unique perspective that helped me consider things I hadn't thought of!

Kalene – Thank you for your many conversations, enthusiasm, insistence on making the Happiness Soldiers™ community be all it can be, and willingness to endorse me and this book!

Margi – Thank you for helping putting some of the initial words down on paper!

Margie & Bill – Thank you for being great supporters all around and for your editing and cover input!

Paula – Thank you for going all out to do every experience, using your colored pencils, and sharing your excitement!

Puvindren – Thank you for your concise feedback, excitement, and willingness to share it with others!

Sue – Thank you for your encouragement, enthusiasm, and help! Your curiosity got me started!

Tina – Thank you for your comical feedback! It was very enjoyable making your suggested changes! I really appreciate your analytical eye, perspective, and conversations!

Shane – My biggest supporter! You always support me in everything I do and am, especially in following my happiness! What didn't you help with? You supported me with encouragement, patience, a critical eye, clarifying ideas, and editing over and over. You created the Happiness Soldiers™ idea, the logo/badge, and the cover. I am so lucky to have you in my life, and I plan on keeping you forever!

TABLE OF CONTENTS

PREFACE

> "The purpose of the universe is the expansion of happiness."
>
> *Deepak Chopra*

The purpose of this book is to expand happiness and hopefully have a little fun while doing so. ☺ If life were perceived as a game that we chose to participate in, perhaps the goal would be to rediscover what we are at our core while existing in a body that adds complexity, need, and desire to the mix. Happiness is tied to your authentic self: the you who exists at your core. Happiness is present *now* in *this* and *every* moment. Everyone is different and so is each person's happiness! No one can define your happiness; you have to discover it for yourself. Happiness is for everyone!

This is not a step-by-step guide. Instead, it is simply another (and perhaps new-to-you) perspective to help you apply your beliefs and values to embrace your individual happiness. This is also not a prescriptive "how to" book or book full of definitive research. This book was written to help people internalize happiness and help them move from average existence to a choice-filled, limitless, authentic state. This is NOT targeted at people who are in crisis. It is for the person who may currently exist without a lot of meaning or purpose. However, that does not necessarily mean that its usefulness is limited to only people who fit this description. The following world views have been incorporated into this book: 1) people are mostly good and 2) abundance is available to all.

At the end of each chapter, there are a set of experiences (or exercises) that you can engage in. The experiences are meant to capture the main learning points from the chapter and be more applicable to learners who don't learn most effectively by reading. This book is designed so you can do the parts that you want to do. If you just want to read, that's an option. However, if you don't want to read and only want to do an experience or multiple experiences, that is also a great option. Feel free to do what works for you and makes you happiest. Completing multiple experiences and having some repetition might help you, but it might also be distracting.

I will consider this book a success if just one person is positively impacted. However, my ultimate goal is to create a culture of happiness where people seek their individual happiness and design their lives around that, and this in turn makes those who aren't seeking it curious enough to seek their own happiness. Hopefully this book can help you choose to make happiness your purpose, aim for your happiness goal, and inspire others by always expanding your happiness!

I implore you to help me create an environment that encourages others in their pursuit of happiness by being a person who is curious and purposeful in embracing your own happiness – it should be fun! If this book doesn't expand your happiness and generate a little fun, use it to make paper airplanes or something else that does!

Fight for, protect, and defend your happiness and help others do the same every day. Become a Happiness Soldier™ today!

CHAPTER 1

WHAT IS HAPPINESS?

Happiness is a state of being. Perhaps you use "joy" or another word to have the same meaning. Whatever word you use, this book will be using "happiness," and you can substitute your word if you like throughout. Again, this book should add to your happiness and be fun for you! **Happiness is a choice!** It is a choice that is made continually. Don't kid yourself; not making this or any other choice *is* making a choice (to NOT make a choice)!

So what is happiness? Many people only associate "true" happiness with special events or circumstances, such as having a baby, getting married, partying, or winning a championship match. These special (or similar) moments can cause a temporary huge spike in happiness (the words bliss and ecstasy might come to mind), but that spike is not sustainable and too quickly fades. Bliss is bound by circumstance and circumstantial bliss is, at best, temporary. On the other hand, everyday happiness is enduring and can make these blissful moments even more fulfilling. If you think that happiness is something you mostly get from external sources, you might want to reconsider. Happiness comes from within an individual and is sustained and expanded by living authentically and purposefully. Are you wondering if happiness has somehow skipped you or someone you know? Nope…everyone exists to be happy…a very individualized happiness. Abundance doesn't have a limit for those embracing happiness! We were created to be happy and to seek happiness.

No matter where you are in life, it's where you're supposed to be. You can choose to accept happiness at any point in time.

Keep in mind that happiness should not be compared and is not bound by perfection or expectations. Happiness also isn't "keeping up with the Joneses" or anyone else on your block or in your life. Think about it. You have probably met someone who seems to have everything but isn't happy. On the other hand, you may know of someone who has very little in terms of possessions yet is very happy. The greatest happiness you can find is internal. When internal happiness is your guiding force, you're on the right track. Challenge yourself to find and value the vast well of happiness inside you. Enduring happiness isn't received from external possessions or from others. However, upon embracing your internal happiness, external sources can definitely add to it. Your internal happiness is like the ice cream and syrup of your sundae while external happiness can add the whipped cream and cherry on top.

Want a bit of good news? Happiness attracts happiness. It is *not* selfish to embrace your happiness; rather, embracing your happiness allows you to not only give more of your true, authentic, purposeful self to those you most care about but also to have the impact that only you can have. Consider that refusing to embrace your happiness limits your value and purpose in life and can discourage others you care about from stepping into their happiness.

What would change if you made happiness your purpose? Would the wonderful individual that you are shine a little more and undertake more projects or relationships that you have been putting off? Would you give yourself permission to be different or outstanding as only you can be?

It can be challenging for some people to initially ponder happiness. What you currently have is a known. What risk are you willing to take to go after something new and uncertain? How many of those around you will cheer you on, and how many will do everything they can to keep you exactly where you are? They may fear that you may not have a use for them when you go down your happiness path, or they may not want to take any risks themselves to try to step up to their potential and be more in line with their own happiness journey. Wouldn't it be easier if there were

4

a tribe or collection of people just waiting to welcome in the next person who chooses his/her happiness.

All that said, it can be easier to find and embrace happiness when it's a culture you are already surrounded by. However, if this isn't your situation, you can be aware and make conscious choices to make your situation better suited for you and your happiness. One way to do this is to encourage others in their search for happiness and inspire them to be curious about their happiness. Demonstrating your happiness is a great way to pique others' curiosity. People may ask themselves "what is different about her?" and discover something new about themselves. Don't minimize the value of this single act!

We are all so unique, so why wouldn't our happiness be just as unique? For example, my purpose and values are highly aligned with fun, spontaneity, and play. If I were to know everything (or even just a little bit sometimes), this would greatly hinder my ability to play in the unknown and to be somewhat flippantly spontaneous. These are things I really enjoy, and they define me in many ways. For me, I don't care to know more than what I need to know to have happiness. Many of you may be more analytical, may enjoy the known and predictable, and may want to understand the why's of everything. I am thankful you are that way! All of us exist as we are, and we are lucky that we are created in such variety! Can you imagine how boring our existence would be without that variety? This same variety should bleed into our idea of what happiness can be for each individual and make it more acceptable for our individual happiness to shine through.

Whether it becomes more acceptable or not, you must choose to accept your unique happiness...no one is just like you! You control nothing except for your choice, and that's why choice is so precious. Figure out the best way to use your choice. Choose to take ownership of your own happiness. No one else can do that for you without imposing their own idea of happiness on you. Once you choose to accept happiness, it lives in constant expansion by your choice. Happiness will shine through you, and others will see it and be curious to know what it is for them. I believe emphatically that you have limitless potential, and you are meant to have happiness. Don't wait and take this for granted, though. Life is short; take ownership of your happiness today! Accept that you are exactly where you are supposed to be at this moment! ☺

EXPERIENCES

Experience A:

1) Find and correct/fill in where the shapes ("X", triangle, oval, star, checkmark, diamond, arrow, lighting bolt, heart) were stamped into the below statement.

2) Put a frame around the below statement.

3) Write or draw what your happiness is around the frame you have created.

Experience B:

1) Visualize for yourself what "happiness is my choice" means to you.

2) Draw a picture, icon, or symbol to represent the meaning to you. Make sure when you look at it, it reminds you of the happiness you pictured before.

Experience C:

1) Tear out a blank piece of paper from the back of this book (or from any notebook).

2) Tear it into the shape of a capital "H".

3) Decorate your capital "H" with words and symbols of your happiness.

Experience D:

1) Analyze the below quote.

Better to do something imperfectly than to do nothing flawlessly. ~ Robert H. Schuller

2) How can this quote be applied to your happiness?

3) What, if anything, would you change about the quote to better apply it to your happiness?

Experience E:

1) Read, sing, or rap the below quote out loud.

   Optimism is a strategy for making a better future. Because unless you believe that the future can be better, you are unlikely to step up and take responsibility for making it so. ~ Noam Chomsky

2) Say aloud to yourself or tell a friend how this applies to your happiness being your choice.

3) Say aloud to yourself or tell a friend how you can better apply this to your life.

CHAPTER 2
STUCK IN NEUTRAL

There are a variety of perceptions in life, ranging from the highly positive to the extremely negative. It may seem obvious, but it's worth stating that a positive perception of, and outlook on, life is the best for happiness. Positive people are typically happiness seekers. In contrast, negative people are basically negative to themselves, not purposefully harming others, but choosing to let life happen to them while complaining and being disgruntled that life isn't fair or how it should be. In between positive and negative is neutral. Although it is better than negative, neutral still is not a recipe for happiness.

Neutral people go through the motions of existing. However, they are not really present. These people can be comfortable with their lives but put little to no effort in raising their happiness level. They may not see happiness as a goal, as a possibility, or as something worthy of effort. For these and many other reasons, they do not make progress in their happiness journey. They may have momentary or short-lived happiness, but they would rather give up their choice (which we know *is* a choice) than get off the fence. Happiness may seem like too much effort, so it's not a priority for them to choose it. In case you haven't realized yet, I am here to encourage those on the neutral fence to take the leap toward happiness. ☺

Many of us know someone who is in a relationship that doesn't match up to his/her values or beliefs. Yet, the person would rather ignore looking closer at the situation than to confirm anything that might change or even end the relationship. In these cases, the people may think that it is better to "have" the relationship the way it is than to not have it at all. An alternative possibility is that the relationship could flourish by it being better aligned with both people's values and beliefs. This is a situation where the person probably thought he/she didn't want to make a choice, but in truth he/she was making a continuous choice to stay in the situation and avoid looking into it more. Do you want to be comfortable with the status quo and not know what you really desire? If so, why is that? My guess is broaching this subject will change your comfort level with the situation. Seeking your greatest happiness or believing in your potential is all in your court!

People in neutral may feel they are always being judged. They may also be people pleasers. Life is happening *to* them, not because of them or with any input from them (again, this is their perception). Neutral happens by default and can be associated with a lack of accountability. Get out of neutral by *choosing*. Use your choice, potential, and efforts to create the reality you want. One cool thing about intentionally choosing is that you get to choose again and again. You can change your path at any time. Are you thinking this makes you inconsistent, volatile, and irresponsible? Another viewpoint is that it makes you flexible, loyal to yourself and your happiness, as well as inspirational. You have the opportunity and ability to expand your perspective!

In hindsight, even initial so-called "bad" choices can lead to creating more happiness as long as you stay present and keep using your choice to move in the direction you desire. An example of this is going to college for a degree that your parents expect you to get when you just really want to work on diesel engines or be a hair stylist. Conceivably, during the experience, you could meet your future spouse, learn something that changes your mind in the process, or become even more committed to being what you wanted in the first place. Choice creates energy and motion. Your choice exists at every moment during the experience of life! Use it! The experience resulting from a choice can get you closer to happiness, so make another choice *today*.

EXPERIENCES

Experience A:

1) In the below diagram, decorate/complete the stick figures to represent the states they are in.

2) In the below diagram, draw or write what would be attracted to the limbs and/or bodies of each stick figure as they exist in their assigned state (Negative, Neutral, and Positive).

3) In the below diagram, circle where you currently see yourself, and put a star where you want to be.

Negative Person

Neutral Person

Positive Person

Experience B:

1) Imagine a person in a Negative state. Draw a picture, icon, or symbol that reminds you of what you visualized.

2) Imagine a person in a Neutral state. Draw a picture, icon, or symbol that reminds you of what you visualized.

3) Imagine a person in a Positive state. Draw a picture, icon, or symbol that reminds you of what you visualized.

4) Circle the picture, icon, or symbol you drew in the above steps that represents where you are at right now.

5) Visualize what your most positive state would look like, and create your symbol to remember what you pictured.

Experience C:

1) Tear out a blank piece of paper from the back of this book (or from any notebook).

2) Tear it into 4 somewhat equal pieces.

3) On one of the 4 pieces write Negative, on the second piece write Neutral, and on the third piece write Positive.

4) Place these 3 pieces with the words Negative, Neutral, and Positive around the room.

5) Tear the remaining blank fourth piece into 12 small pieces.

6) Take 4 of the small pieces from Step 5 to the Negative piece. Think or speak an attribute you associate with someone in a negative state. For each attribute you think or speak, throw down a small piece of paper.

7) Take 4 of the small pieces from Step 5 to the Neutral piece. Think or speak an attribute you associate with someone in a neutral state. For each attribute you think or speak, hold a small piece of paper out at shoulder height, and let it drop.

8) Take the last 4 small pieces from Step 5 to the Positive piece. Think or speak an attribute you associate with someone in a positive state. For each attribute you think or speak, toss a small piece of paper up in the air.

9) Go stand by the state you associate with yourself.

10) Grab the piece of paper with the state you are standing by and take it to the Positive paper, if you aren't already there. Tear the paper in your hand into 12 pieces, and toss the small pieces of paper up in the air.

Experience D:

1) Analyze the below quotes.

As we let our own light shine we unconsciously allow others to do the same.
~ Marianne Williamson

NEGATIVE PERSON

I have begun everything with the idea that I could succeed, and I never had much patience with the multitudes of people who are always ready to explain why one cannot succeed. ~ Booker T. Washington

NEUTRAL PERSON

When one door closes another door opens; but we so often look so long and so regretfully upon the closed door, that we do not see the ones which open for us.
~ Alexander Graham Bell

POSITIVE PERSON

Death is not the greatest loss in life. The greatest loss is what dies inside us while we live. ~ Norman Cousins

2) Draw a line from each of the above quotes to the state you most associate it with - Negative, Neutral, or Positive. Have at least one quote assigned to each state.

3) Circle the quote you most associate with yourself.

4) Modify a quote or write your own quote representing your most positive state.

Experience E:

1) Use funny voices, whisper, and/or use a foreign accent to read the below quotes out loud.

Most people would rather be certain they're miserable, than risk being happy. ~ Robert Anthony

We don't view complexity as a necessary evil. We see it as a thief that must be apprehended.
~ Alan Siegel and Irene Etzkorn

He who fights with monsters might take care lest he thereby become a monster. And if you gaze for long into an abyss, the abyss gazes also into you. ~ Friedrich Nietzsche

Progress happens one step at a time. It begins with knowing that we may not always control the circumstances around us, but we always have total control over our perception of those circumstances. ~ Joe Calloway

He who trims himself to suit everyone will soon whittle himself away. ~ Raymond Hull

2) Pick a quote that you most associate with a negative person/state and write Negative by it. Repeat the quote aloud in a sad voice.

3) Pick a quote that you most associate with a neutral person/state and write Neutral by it. Repeat the quote aloud in a monotone voice.

4) Pick a quote that you most associate with a positive person/state and write Positive by it. Repeat the quote aloud in an upbeat voice.

5) Circle the quote that best represents where you are now. Use a voice that represents your choice, and read it aloud.

6) What song would express what your most positive state would be?

7) Sing your favorite part of the song.

CHAPTER 3

ACCEPT HAPPINESS

Happiness is a state that already exists. It is your choice whether to inhabit it or not. If you haven't already done so, here is your official life-long invitation to make happiness your internal state.

There are no roadblocks to your baseline happiness once you embrace it, because it's not a journey; it's where you already are right now. It is where you start. This level of happiness is not something to earn, achieve, or acquire. It is already completely available to you…you already have it, and it's just begging you to recognize its existence inside you. You just need to accept it and embrace it. You have life…therefore, you are worthy of happiness!

You have happiness at your foundation now. Don't think you have to wait for when you get married (or divorced), when you have a certain amount of money, when you get that perfect job, or any other arbitrary experience which *may* happen someday. Additionally, don't expect any person, event, condition, or circumstance to create a better time than the present for you to accept what is always there to be freely received.

Accepting happiness is the starting point. This is the first step in establishing a baseline from which to build. So, what are you waiting for? It's a simple choice of saying "yes, I accept happiness!" Allow yourself to feel excitement and relief as you experience this new development. If you are hesitant not knowing what this will create, realize that you always have a choice and can change your path or scrap the concept whenever you want. Why wait? Step into happiness right now!

EXPERIENCES

Experience A:

1) Create your personal happiness logo below.

2) If you were to incorporate a tagline into your logo, what would it be?

3) What, if anything, is still stopping you from accepting happiness?

4) If you were to explain to someone by sketching a comic strip about what it was like to accept your happiness, what would it look like?

Experience B:

1) Sit in silence with a smile on your face for 10 seconds.

2) Visualize what the below statements mean to you for 30 seconds each.

I, myself, am enough to have happiness.

My choice is important to my happiness.

It is possible to be happy in any circumstance.

I choose the life I have and will create the life I want.

Everything is as it should be.

Happiness is a state of being.

I'm invited to have happiness.

3) What did you picture?

4) What more, if anything, do you need to reframe to internalize your baseline happiness?

Experience C:

1) Tear a blank piece of paper from the back of this book (or from any notebook).

2) Tear the paper into 10 pieces.

3) Write a number on each piece between 1 and 5. You can instead use a 6-sided dice if you prefer.

4) Start at one end of the room (or yard if you are outside). Your goal is to go across the room or yard.

5) In order to move on your turn, you will need to name something that will help you to accept happiness in the now. The same answer can only be used once.

6) After you say it out loud, choose a piece of paper from your pile, or roll the die.

7) The number you choose or roll is the number of steps you get to take toward the other side of the room or yard. For more fun, try a different method of movement each time you choose or roll a number. For example, your first time – walk; your second time – skip; your third time – hop; your fourth time – waddle…and so on. Feel free to be creative!

8) When you get across the room or yard, state what you need to accept happiness, if anything. Write it down in your book, and write down when you are going to get it.

Experience D:

1) Put the following words in each sentence in the correct order to complete the quote by Will Garcia:

Acceptance step change toward the first is.

Door once yourself, open change you accept the you to.

All you do that's have to.

You it's change is do, something allow not you something.

2) What does this quote mean for your happiness?

The first step toward change is acceptance. Once you accept yourself, you open the door to change. That's all you have to do. Change is not something you do, it's something you allow.
~ Will Garcia

Experience E:

1) Fill in the blanks in the below quote with the following words. Use each word only once.

error   critic   strong   worthy   face

victory   timid   daring   strive

It is not the _____ who counts; not the man who points out how the _____ man stumbles, or where the doer of deeds could have done them better. The credit belongs to the man who is actually in the arena, whose _____ is marred by dust and sweat and blood; who strives valiantly; who errs, who comes short again and again, because there is no effort without _____ and shortcoming; but who does actually _____ to do the deeds; who knows great enthusiasms, the great devotions; who spends himself in a _____ cause; who at the best knows in the end the triumph of high achievement, and who at the worst, if he fails, at least fails while _____ greatly, so that his place shall never be with those cold and _____ souls who neither know _____ nor defeat.

~ Theodore Roosevelt

2) Read the quote out loud while covering your ears tightly.
3) Listen to what your heart says in silence.
4) Write down what you heard, and repeat it back to yourself aloud.

5) How can this quote apply to happiness?

CHAPTER 4
A HAPPINESS MINDSET

Life isn't always rainbows and butterflies…isn't that great? If you want to appreciate a rainbow more, you can't always have rainbows, or they become too commonplace and lose their luster. Yes, you can of course add some glitter to the rainbow to create a new dimension to consider! ☺ A mindset of happiness includes knowing that life would lack excitement and be uninteresting without challenges and differences. Happiness on a daily basis necessitates you willingly inserting yourself into situations that are challenging and different and finding the possibilities and opportunities that are present; this is happiness at the speed of life. Having this attitude is worthwhile and allows you to more easily navigate your happiness journey.

A positive attitude is an underlying key to having a happiness mindset. It might be fragile in the beginning, but over time it can become a very resilient habit. You have to desire it and go after it knowing that you are worthy. Accept that life happens and that everything isn't always what you want it to be. Reframe mistakes and failure to be useful to your happiness. They can just be another form of data. They can be useful in this manner. Accept your mistakes as opportunities for learning, and redefine them; recalibrate your mindset. You might experience setbacks on your journey. If you aren't ready to redefine them, then you can at least concede that as a human being, you make mistakes, and there's no way to completely avoid them. Accept that imperfect isn't bad…it's perfect! No one is perfect, so start each day with a clean slate. What can you create today?

Reset to your happiness mindset every day! Are you surprised that your mindset is also tied to your choice? I'm trusting that you will see choice is a common theme throughout this book and give it the value that it deserves.

In many job interviews, the interviewers ask "what are your strengths and weaknesses?" If your mindset is that you have strengths and weaknesses, you might be prepared to answer this question. Conversely, if your mindset is that I am the way I am and everything about me can be a strength, then it depends on the situation as to whether others consider your actions/traits to be strengths or not. For example, someone might be considered detail-oriented and be a great accountant by making sure the books match to the cent, but this same level of detail might be considered obsessive and inappropriate if someone mowing a field went back with a ruler to ensure that every piece of grass was mowed to the exact same length. Another example is someone in sales being persistent in reaching out to potential customers to get meetings set up. This same persistence might be considered stubborn in other situations and be considered a weakness. Having the mindset that the situation determines the value of your strengths changes your perception and opens up opportunities and possibilities that didn't exist before. Adjusting the mindset you have about happiness can do the same thing for you.

Another mindset adjustment you can make is to not tolerate life impeding your happiness…it wants you to have happiness…find your path! Happiness increases resilience, making you more nimble, mobile, and less stunned when uncertainty creeps in. Accept happiness, and reflect a happiness mindset by having an attitude of happiness regardless of external circumstances. Be more positive with an attitude of opportunity and possibility. You can maintain and grow your happiness even when everything isn't all smiles and fun. Make life as much fun as you can even during challenging moments. If you feel like you've moved away from happiness, you can choose to adjust your path at any time because your happiness journey is agile and ever-changing.

A happiness mindset gives a different texture to the world. Your baseline happiness will gradually rise over time as you maintain your happiness mindset. Be aware that your attitude change doesn't necessarily make others' attitudes toward you better; nevertheless, stay true to your new charted course.

EXPERIENCES

Experience A:

1) Let's make some lemonade! You will need to find the possible parts of a happiness mindset below. For each possible part of a happiness mindset, draw an ingredient for your lemonade to surround the words. The ingredients are lemons, sugar, ice, water and a little bit of love.☺ Use each ingredient only once. Put an "X" through the words that aren't possible parts of a happiness mindset.

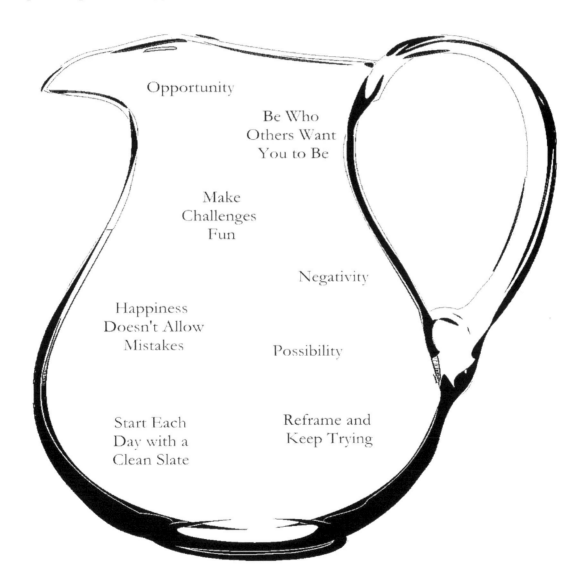

2) What will be your greatest challenge in maintaining your happiness mindset?

3) What is the best way for you to remind yourself to drink some of the lemonade you just made in all situations?

Experience B:

1) Envision something you find a little unpleasant such as a meeting, being around an unpleasant person, paying taxes, or something else.

2) Now, imagine how you will maintain your happiness mindset knowing you will be in that situation at some point.

3) Challenging situations occur throughout life. What can you picture in your mind to remind you of your happiness mindset during challenging situations?

Experience C:

1) Tear out a blank piece of paper from the back of the book (or from any notebook).

2) Tear it into 8 pieces.

3) On 4 pieces of paper, write an attribute/quality/characteristic (examples can be: hard-working, excitable, detail-oriented, etc.). Shuffle the pieces, and put them in a pile.

4) On the other 4 pieces of paper, write "strength" or "weakness". Shuffle the pieces, and put them in their own pile.

5) Keep the two piles separated.

6) Pick one attribute/quality/characteristic randomly from its pile, and pick a strength or weakness piece randomly from its pile.

7) Act out a situation using the drawn attribute/quality/characteristic while considering how others may see it as a strength or weakness (determined from the "strength" or "weakness" piece you also drew).

8) Repeat Steps 6-7 until all the pieces in each pile have been used.

9) If you have extra time and want to do more, you can draw the attributes again and act out the opposite situation (if you acted it as a strength, then you would now act it as a weakness or vice versa).

Experience D:

1) For each of the below situations that could be framed as mistakes and failures, instead write how the situation could to be useful to you and your happiness.

Situation	Reframed Useful Mindset/ Positive Spin to Situation
You're late.	_____ _____
You didn't get the promotion you expected.	_____ _____
You got bad news from the doctor.	_____ _____
You were fired.	_____ _____
Your friend canceled lunch with you.	_____ _____
You got your neighbor's mail in your mailbox.	_____ _____
You were cut off in traffic.	_____ _____
You're going to a family event that you usually don't enjoy.	_____ _____
You forgot to run the errand you agreed to do.	_____ _____

2) What patterns, if any, did you notice?

3) What situations are the most challenging for you to reframe?

4) Creating a filter for information to get sorted through before it is allowed to impact your happiness can be very useful. What filter can you put in place to make it easier to reframe the situations that are most challenging for you to reframe?

Experience E:

1) Whisper aloud the below quotes focused on an attitude of opportunity and possibility.

By replacing fear of the unknown with curiosity we open ourselves up to an infinite stream of possibility. ~ Alan Watts

Security is not the meaning of my life. Great opportunities are worth the risk. ~ Shirley Hufstedler

If you concentrate on finding whatever is good in every situation, you will discover that your life will suddenly be filled with gratitude, a feeling that nurtures the soul. ~ Rabbi Harold Kushner

You can't go back and make a new start, but you can start right now and make a brand new ending. ~ James R. Sherman

2) Now, in a resolute voice, confidently declare the words of the one quote that most speaks to you of possibility and opportunities.

3) What sound(s) do you associate with possibility and opportunity?

4) What does your happiness mindset say or sound like? Say it out loud.

CHAPTER 5

EXPANDING HAPPINESS

Happiness has unlimited expansion potential. There are many ways to expand your happiness, and they can be very specific to each individual. For me, it's showing up with a positive attitude, watching happy movies, playing with my nieces and nephew, and listening to upbeat music among other things. It's also limiting my exposure to and acceptance of things that don't add to my happiness, such as watching violent movies or the news, spending time with negative or indifferent people, and internalizing negative comments on social media. Spending more time in the present is extremely helpful for my happiness. When did you last purposely spend time to be fully present, in the now? I have taken up meditation to help with this along with ignoring my phone while I'm involved in an activity or with another person. Expanding happiness can also be making sure happiness is the focus in more parts of your life. So, expanding your happiness is again, you guessed it, your choice!

Creating a filter for information to get sorted through before it is allowed to impact your happiness can be very useful. One way to do this is to ask yourself some simple questions. *Will this help add to my happiness?* This is the question I'm constantly asking myself. *How does this move me towards my happiness?* The questions can be even more helpful if they are personalized to your happiness journey.

There are times when others are frustrated by something, and they explain their frustration to me. What goes through my mind is *will internalizing their frustration add to my happiness? If it won't, what will?* Perhaps it would be best to ask them a question about possibilities or opportunities in the situation to expand their mind frame or to provide a resource. In a few cases, just listening to the person increased my happiness by helping him/her to let go of the frustration altogether.

As adults, we might get frustrated with having dandelions in our manicured lawns. On the other hand, my nieces go searching for and get super excited to find dandelions to blow the fluffy white tops off of and to make flower bouquets. Consider tapping into your inner kid. How can you incorporate play, creativity, or a game into your life? What were your favorite things to do as a kid? Challenge yourself to add creativity to your life. Don't worry about the results…the effort is what counts and what you control. The journey is what matters! How can you feed your inner kid today?

As a salesperson, it can be a challenge to keep reaching out to people if you think you are bugging or bothering the people you are contacting. However, you could make this a bit more fun by turning this challenge into a game. Perhaps your reframed goal is to reach out with the intention of helping the person with whatever they need (not just convincing the person that he/she needs what you are offering). If the person happens to need what you offer, then that's great. However, if the person doesn't have a need for what you offer, then you can maybe be helpful by providing him/her another resource instead. The game can be to congratulate yourself for actually receiving a certain number of "no's" everyday knowing that you tried to help every person who gave you a "no." This is an example of making something a game and staying focused on your efforts.

Another way to expand happiness is to consider the mystery in the uncertainty and the unknown that we live in as something necessary and even fun. To accept that you don't know and that perhaps you're not supposed to know and that's just exactly how it's supposed to be can help transform the way you live and your perspective. Have you ever interacted with a person who never looks forward to Mondays? When I meet these people, I always remind them that Mondays make up about 14% (or one seventh) of their lives…seems like a lot of life to automatically undervalue to me. If you're surrounding yourself with toxic people or situations, consider what

58

that's doing for you and how that is or isn't adding to your happiness. Spoiler alert: they're most likely bad for you and your happiness journey. Surrounding yourself with people who strive for their unique happiness can make your happiness journey expand more easily.

Be cautious in trying to measure your happiness. For some, this has potential to decrease happiness rather than expand it. Instead, expand your happiness by being grateful in your daily life! Appreciating even the smallest things in your life can help you put a positive spin on life and add to your happiness. Choose to make it your habit to pause and count your blessings on a daily basis. Some people are upset when they get lemons, and others are grateful they have an ingredient for lemonade. It's your choice what type of person you want to be!

Growing happiness for some people eventually requires venturing outside of their current comfort zone and eventually growing their comfort zone. You may need to challenge yourself in order to expand your comfort zone. The more comfortable you get with uncertainty, with the unknown, and with accepting and embracing things as they are, the more you will attract happiness to yourself. This also helps you to be resilient with your happiness when surprise situations occur.

We each have our unique strengths and idea of happiness. I for one am not the traveling type. You know them...people who are excited to go see new or renowned places any chance they get at the drop of a hat. To me, traveling to see "cool things" or beautiful places has never stacked up in comparison to having an ice cream cone or going on a walk with the people I most like to be around. Now, if these people happened to be at that beautiful place or seeing those "cool things," I would want to be there with them. For the traveling type, this may not be the case...and that is just perfect! Just another way that happiness is unique to the individual. Having a greater awareness of the many forms happiness takes can make it easier to expand your own happiness.

Happiness has many diverse appearances and can incorporate numerous seemingly contrary behaviors. My outward happiness existence can be seen in my dancing, smiling, laughing loudly, childlike play, and high energy movements. At other times, it could be less apparent in my relaxed snuggling of my loved ones or baby animals or reading a book or manga. Sitting forward (but watching my posture of course) while having a meaningful conversation with a few people is another dimension of my visible happiness existence. For others, you may see a sparkle in their eyes while touring a beautiful region on horseback or contemplation or excitement in their voice or face while tinkering with a car or electronic device. A passion experienced while painting, a lightness or bounce while organizing, or singing or humming in all that you do are just a few more ways that happiness can shine through. Recognizing and embracing your unique happiness can bolster and expand your happiness to a new level.

Focusing on your unique strengths and idea of happiness can help you create more opportunities and possibilities in your life. If you're a person who wants something in the future, what can you do to have part of it today or in the very near future? For example, if you want to travel when you retire, see what type of day trip you can take right now. If you want to start or resume a hobby, what can you do today to start on that path? Focusing on what you can do now, in the present, instead of the past or the future, can also increase your awareness of yourself and your happiness.

EXPERIENCES

Experience A:

1) Sketch your happiness in each of the below scenarios (ideas: excitement, reading a book, contentment at the beach, playing with a dog, tinkering with a computer, interacting with new people, etc.).

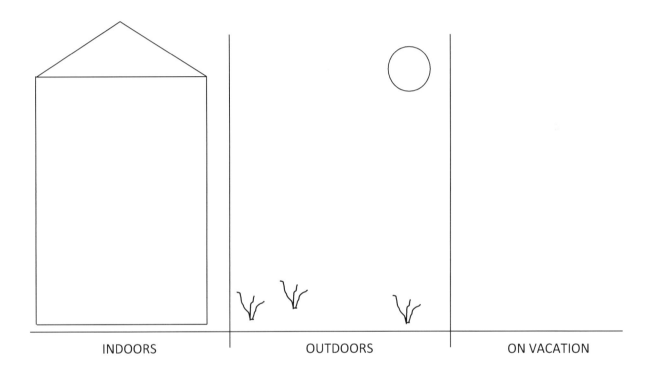

INDOORS   OUTDOORS   ON VACATION

2) What can you do to further expand your happiness in other or more parts of your life and internally (ideas: health, work, family, spirituality, socially, in the morning, at night, when with people, when by yourself, etc.)?

Experience B:

1) Visualize your ideal future. Where are you? Who is around you? What are you feeling?

2) Picture in your mind what you can do to have some or more of your ideal future today or in the near future.

3) Imagine your priorities in life.

4) Insert your ideal future into your imagined priorities.

5) What will you do to keep your ideal future a high priority for yourself?

Experience C:

1) Consider the below quote.

When you're focused upon how good the good is, the good gets better. ~ Abraham Hicks

2) Tear a blank piece of paper out of the back of the book (or from any notebook).

3) Tear it into 6 pieces.

4) On each of the 6 pieces of paper, write something you are grateful for.

5) Put the pieces into a pile.

6) Draw a piece from the pile.

7) Read what you are grateful for aloud.

8) While you wad the piece of paper into a ball, say or think about what you are going to do to appreciate what you wrote you are grateful for even more.

9) Draw another piece from the pile.

10) Read what you are grateful for aloud.

11) Add the piece of paper to the outside of your small ball, and scrunch it together to make a larger ball. Say or think about what you are going to do to appreciate what you wrote you are grateful for even more.

12) Repeat Steps 9-11 until there are no pieces left in the pile.

Experience D:

1) In the below table (it is below Step 3), list three (A, B, & C) topics or areas that you most want to be more comfortable with in the "Topic/Area I Want To Be More Comfortable With" column (examples: approaching people, telling people "no", speaking in public, giving myself "me time", being different/myself, showing gratitude, asking questions, listening, doing what makes me happy, etc.).

2) Complete the "My Ideal Comfort Zone Someday" column in the below table by writing what your ideal state/reality is for each topic/area you listed.

3) Complete the "A Little Outside My Current Comfort Zone" column in the below table by writing something you can try that feels safe but that also pushes a boundary/assumption you have.

Topic/Area I Want To Be More Comfortable With	My Ideal Comfort Zone Someday	A Little Outside My Current Comfort Zone
A) _____ _____	_____ _____	_____ _____
B) _____ _____	_____ _____	_____ _____
C) _____ _____	_____ _____	_____ _____

4) Consider the following: What is experimentation? Experimentation can be used to collect data when you make a change to the way you currently do something. With the right mindset, there is no failure when experimenting…only data. You can use the data you collect from each experiment to determine the next experiment you want to do. It is a way to test the waters while having a lifejacket. Experimenting is important since it is a way to redefine success as the act of carrying out an experiment instead of getting the

result/outcome you expect. It helps to remove mental blocks and fears and allows progress at a pace that is acceptable to the individual. The goal of experimentation is to keep getting data from which you can make decisions/conclusions instead of existing only in your head with your assumptions and only thinking about what might happen without taking any action to confirm or prove otherwise. You can use the data from each experiment (instead of making assumptions), and then experiment again until you get to your goal. You can introduce small experiments that are safe but that also push a boundary/assumption you have to produce incremental useful change.

5) What experiment are you going to try that is a little outside your current comfort zone but feels safe/achievable?

6) What is your plan to continue expanding your comfort zone to your ideal future state?

Experience E:

1) Read aloud the following: Creating a filter to sort information before it is allowed to impact my happiness can be very useful. One way to do this is to ask yourself some simple questions. An example of a filtering question is: *Will this help add to my happiness?*

2) Create and say out loud your own filtering questions using each of the below words to start your questions?

What…

How…

Who…

When…

Which…

Why…

3) Say aloud the question that resonates most with your idea of safeguarding your happiness.

4) Repeat the question you resonate with in Step 3 in a voice of someone you respect 5 times.

CHAPTER 6
THE NATURE OF HAPPINESS

Sometimes I get the pleasure of reading my niece a book before bed. She chose a mermaid book recently. As we were reading it, when the mermaids were mentioned or there was a picture of them, she would say "they aren't real." Thinking back on it, instead of saying "right," how many more possibilities would have been created if I had said "but what if they were?" What does it hurt for her to know the truth but still play with ideas and be creative?

We are born with the natural desire to play, laugh at the simplest things, and be creative. Children are typically bundles of joy, so it seems to be a natural state that is somehow affected as we age and as society and outside influences impact us.

Finding, accepting, maintaining, and expanding your happiness can seem selfish. The relentless pursuit of happiness can seem or feel selfish too, and others may make you feel that way as well. This may be one of your toughest challenges on your happiness journey. It may take some time to feel comfortable or find comfort in thinking that everyone should be pursuing their happiness. There's nothing selfish about it! If everyone were pursuing their individual happiness, then the world would be a better place. The greater good is served by people pursuing their happiness.

Having a purpose or meaning to life can give you reason to exist, create, use your gifts, and tap into your highest potential. We are born to be happy! You are unique, extraordinary, wanted, full of potential, and gifted with choice! Don't internalize the endless monotony that sometimes surrounds us! Instead, be your authentic self and impact this world in the way that only you can! Everything is how it should be. Make your mark, and reach for the impossible!

Sometimes looking for your purpose is your purpose at the moment. Speed bumps are put into play to keep life interesting. Curious speed bumps, such as a person offering you a job that doesn't match what you want to do with your life, can occur frequently to keep you on your toes. Things can move and change very quickly when you are aligned with your authentic self and your purposeful happiness. You may have seen this happen to others and thought they are just so lucky.

Average people aren't thinking everyday about their purpose, greater surroundings, or divine power. They are more concerned or worried about how others perceive what they're doing, getting acceptance from others, matching up to their peers, or meeting their parents' or others' expectations (or *perceived* expectations). You can never make everyone happy. Instead, you can purposely pursue happiness for yourself, and encourage others to do the same for themselves. Consider trying to take actions that you can control…at least until the day that worrying makes situations better. (Spoiler alert #2: that day will never come.)

Your individual happiness is not the same as any other person's individual happiness, and other people don't always want what's best for you in the first place. Finding a person who supports your best self and your happiness in the way that is most useful to you is very rare. It's very difficult to surround yourself with only people who want what you want for yourself. In many cases, people try to bring you down in order for them to feel better instead of everybody lifting each other up so that everybody is in a higher state. Don't fall into the trap that many others are falling into. If you have, acknowledge it, and use your choice to make it what you want it to be.

Most people would rather not know than risk getting the answer they don't want at that moment. If everybody were confident that they were going to affirm their situation, confirm their beliefs, or

74

get confirmation that what they're doing is the right thing or the best thing, they would be more likely to question what they are doing. But if they fear that the result of that analysis is going to tell them to change everything (or even one important thing), then they're less likely to do it.

People who are purposeful resist this situation more of the time. That's because their purpose is so important to them that by hindering themselves they hinder their purpose. These types of people may never find comfort living in the dark and would rather get an answer they may not want or like. It's uncomfortable to them to be comfortable when not on a purposeful track.

For many, realization of their highest happiness is tied to knowing that they're a part of something bigger. Spiritual alignment in life can make your happiness journey much clearer, because you can more easily not think that everything is against you, not need to understand everything, and know that things are going as they should. Even if something isn't what you think is right for you, you may have a better chance of thinking that at least it's right for the system/universe. You have a choice to strengthen what the universe wants for you and embrace this flow or choose another path. Happiness is sourced from something…a power greater than yourself! For you, it might show up in creativity, purpose, beauty, thoughtfulness, humor, challenge, achievement, or something else. This source of power wants us to be happy.

EXPERIENCES

Experience A:

1) Sketch your happiness travel bag and contents after considering the following quote:

   He who would travel happily must travel light. ~ Antoine de Saint-Exupéry

2) Narrate the story of one of the below quotes using visuals such as graphics and pictures.

   How does one become a butterfly? … You must want to fly so much that you are willing to give up being a caterpillar. ~ Trina Paulus

   When I let go of what I am, I become what I might be. ~ Lao Tzu

Experience B:

1) Picture what you are a part of that is bigger than you.

2) Imagine the source of your happiness.

3) Read the below quote.

   Playing it safe is the riskiest choice we can ever make. ~ Sarah Ban Breathnach

4) Visualize what "safe" means to you.

5) Imagine your wildest goals being accomplished.

6) Picture how the source of your happiness supports you in reaching your goals.

7) Imagine what your legacy will be.

8) How, if at all, is your idea of "safe" getting in the way or limiting your potential in Steps 5-7?

Experience C:

1) Consider the following quote:

> *Everything you want is out there waiting for you to ask. Everything you want also wants you. But you have to take action to get it. ~ Jules Renard*

2) Walk through/act out the actions you are going to take to incorporate happiness even further throughout your life.

3) Consider the below quote:

> *The reason it's difficult to learn something new is that it will change you into someone who disagrees with the person you used to be. ~ Seth Godin*

4) Act out disagreeing with the person you will be.

5) Now pretend to be the person you will be, and act out disagreeing with the person you are now.

6) Smile! Give yourself a high-five or hug. ☺

Experience D:

1) Contrast nature versus nurture of happiness.

2) Consider the following quote:

> The *ultimate value of life depends upon awareness and the power of contemplation rather than upon mere survival.* ~ *Aristotle*

3) What are you doing beyond mere survival?

4) Study the following quote.

> *I have no special talents. I am only passionately curious.* ~ *Albert Einstein*

5) What can you be more curious about, and how would you show your curiosity?

Experience E:

1) State the following quote in a cheery voice.

   The essence of philosophy is that a man should so live that his happiness shall depend as little as possible on external things. ~ Epictetus

2) Speak aloud the external things that your happiness depends on.

3) Read aloud the below quote as if you are someone in authority.

   All progress has resulted from people who took unpopular positions. ~ Adlai E. Stevenson

4) Say what unpopular position, if any, you are taking to make progress on your happiness.

5) Read aloud the below quote in the voice of your favorite animated character.

   There's only one wrong way to live and that's unhappily. ~ Patrick Elliott

6) Say your response to this quote (from Step 5).

CHAPTER 7

CONCLUSION

Welcome to the last chapter. I hope you had a little fun exploring happiness (even if you made a few origami creatures or paper airplanes)! Although many ideas were presented in this book, none of them need to be right for you. However, I would encourage you to take time to determine what your idea of happiness is.

Let's take this time as a reflection period. You can ask yourself the following questions or some other questions that better speak to you. Feel free to draw, speak, visualize, write, or act out your responses.

Who am I at my core?

What is my personal happiness?

What are my biggest takeaways?

What makes me ready and willing to choose happiness regardless of the consequences?

What more do I need to do to live fully in my happiness?

What is still missing for me to make the progress I want?

What resources do I have or need?

When exactly will I commit to taking action to live more fully in my happiness?

AFTERWORD

This book was written to help people internalize and embody happiness and help them move from average existence to a choice-filled, limitless, authentic state. Consequently, energizing more people to be curious and purposeful in embracing their own happiness optimistically will inspire our culture to encourage others in their pursuit of happiness. Creating a Happiness Revolution led by Happiness Soldiers™ is the ultimate goal!

Ready to be a Happiness Soldier? Join in our Happiness Revolution by visiting www.HappinessSoldiers.com or www.facebook.com/groups/HappinessSoldiers.

This workbook was designed to expand the ways to choose, embrace, and internalize happiness by having multiple experiences available in many different learning forms. Any suggestions you have to improve these experiences or to reach another learning type are appreciated! I am always looking to improve and would love to hear your thoughts and comments!

ABOUT THE AUTHOR

Christina is passionate about empowering others to create the life and legacy they want! She envisions a world that supports people being happy by each person striving to be more and more happy and encouraging others to be happy in their own authentic way. She is the owner of Possibility Lab LLC and provides happiness coaching and facilitation services globally.

She believes in others, listens to her gut, and stays aligned with her life purpose in her daily actions. This helps her be a catalyst to fast-track her clients' personal and business development. Her positive energy and upbeat attitude energize others to do difficult work, improve their confidence, achieve specific desired results, and feel comfortable navigating uncertainty.

In her free time, Christina enjoys playing with her nieces and nephews, learning about different cultures, volunteering, and playing games with friends.

If you are interested in individual happiness coaching or inviting Christina to speak or hold a workshop for your organization, please contact her at christina@possibility-lab.com.

She is enthusiastically hoping that you will connect and start discussions with her on LinkedIn and Facebook. Visit her website at www.possibility-lab.com to learn more. Experiment with Better™ today!

.